D1152287

Design and concept by Silk Pearce
Typeset by Silk Pearce
Illustrated by David Hughes
Printed and bound in Great Britain by JNV Print
Cover and illustrated section printed on Conqueror Laid, Oyster
Text printed on Conqueror 100% Cotton, Soft White

I am indebted to Arjo Wiggins for the impeccable paper; to Jack Pearce
and Rob Steer of Silk Pearce for their creativity and flair; and of
course to David Hughes for his brilliant illustrations. Without these
generous collaborators this book wouldn't exist.

Acknowledgements
My thanks to David Farnsworth, Steve King, Barbara Bapty,
Chris MacLeod, Andy Evans, Philip Rigg, Matt Holland, Julian David
and Lynne Gerlach; to my parents Sheila and Tim Harvey; to my wife,
Heather; and to Naomi Jaffa, Dean Parkin and Michael Laskey of
The Poetry Trust. Thank you. Thank you all very much.
MH

Other titles by Matt Harvey
*Here We Are Then; Songs Sung Sideways; Standing Up to be Counted
Out; Curtains and Other Material*
www.mattharvey.co.uk

The HOLE IN The SUM of MY PARTS

MATT HARVEY

ILLUSTRATIONS David HUGHES

THE POETRY TRUST

Published 2005 by The Poetry Trust
Registered Charity 1102893
The Cut, 9 New Cut, Halesworth, Suffolk IP19 8BY

Copyright © Matt Harvey 2005

Matt Harvey has asserted his right under the Copyright, Designs and Patents Act 1988 to
be identified as the author of this work

Illustrations © David Hughes 2005

No part of this publication may be reproduced, stored in a retrieval system or
transmitted in any form or by any means without prior permission in writing of the
appropriate individual author, nor be otherwise circulated in any form of binding or
cover other than that in which it is published and without a similar condition
including this condition being imposed on the subsequent purchaser.

ISBN 0-9550910-0-4

CONTENTS

for Heather

VERSE FOUND WHILST READING BETWEEN THE LINES OF A LONELY HEARTS AD

I'm looking for a woman. She must be very nice
And made of all the right ingredients – i.e. sugar, starch, spice...

She should be very simple, and similarly kind
And know how to smooth the crinkles in my melancholy mind

She must of course respect me – as many people do –
I don't ask to be worshipped. I only want what's due

She should be nimble on her feet and not get in my way
She should show a lively interest in everything I say

Ideally she'll be fairly bright (but not have gone to college)
All applicants will take a test in basic general knowledge

It goes without my saying that she must just love to cook
And when I lose a sock or tie she must know where to look

But when I lose my temper she will, if she is wise
Let the worst of it blow over – and then apologise

She mustn't put on make-up, unless I take her out
When she's to hold her body steady and not wriggle it about

A word or two about myself? Well, I am what I am –
An ordinary, undemanding, decent sort of man

Just one last thing, to make quite sure I find the perfect wife
The successful applicant will be asked to complete the
                                                    following sentence:

Life...

No human love comes with a guarantee
that it will last forever, and no-one
would dare ask for a short-term warranty.
What's here today tomorrow may be gone.
When you've been left, that's it. You are bereft.
No company will offer personal cover,
no version of Third Party, Fire and Theft
with No Claims Bonus for a long-term lover.
There could be no financial compensation
for love that's lost. It's simply too expensive.
As yet no known form of remuneration
could meet a claim on Fully Comprehensive.
Don't even think of such a policy.
Now, having made that clear – please, marry me.

She said to him, "You're not the man I married.
You've changed," she said, "I hardly recognise
the man who swept me off my feet, who carried
his young bride across the threshold. He was nice.
And kind, and confident. A little brash.
But – what for me back then was the decider –
he had a steady job. Ah, I was rash.
I saw him principally as a provider.
I knew what I desired, not what I needed.
In life you're not recalled from a false start,
you run the race regardless – that's what we did.
I gave my hand before I gave my heart."
She added, then, before he got too worried:
"I love you far more than the man I married."

LET IT BREATHE

One has a duty
to one's inner beauty
to bring it out
and wave it about
a bit.

SPELLCHECK

I've been feeling sleek and furry
since you came and made me whole,
and now I understand why love's
an anagram of vole.

AFTER TWENTY-THREE YEARS OF MARRIAGE
MRS WILKINSON TENTATIVELY ADDRESSES HER
HUSBAND OVER DINNER

"If you'll pardon my asking please tell me the way to your heart
I thought I was on the right track but I made a false start

I followed the manual's advice then I found myself flummoxed
It seems that I can't after all reach it via the stomach

I can't find it by touch and I'm too tired to take it by storm
If I just groped around in the dark would you say when I'm warm?

I've no wish to be crude but I'm thinking perhaps what I mean is
Would you have preferred it if I had tried via the penis?

I'd creep up by moonlight but I'm scared that I'll scare you away
I once tried all night till you asked me to call it a day

Mr Wilkinson, speak to me, I am your wife after all
And I'm asking for help – I invite you to answer my call"

But her husband just sat looking bothered and panicked and pained
Till she wondered aloud "Is there more to be lost here than gained?

For your silence itself is an eloquent form of disclosure
It tells me your heart's nothing like what it said in the brochure

For the record," she added, "I tried, but you squashed my appeal"
Then they both resumed eating their balanced, nutritious
square meal

I felt I needed some curtains, so I went to buy some material from the curtain material shop, or haberdashery. I said to the assistant – a man of about my age, about my height, slightly smarter than me:
"I need some material."
He said, "What's it for?"
"It's for curtains."
"What are the curtains for?"
"They're to keep prying eyes out and warmth in."
"Anything else?"
"Yes, I want them to represent me." I felt myself blushing as I said this, but he said: "Don't be embarrassed. This is a haberdasher's. We get all sorts in here. How do you want them to represent you?"
"I want them to speak of who I am."
"What? To say who you are?"
"No, not to say it directly, but to speak of it. I want something that speaks of who I am. That doesn't shout it, insisting that you hear, but simply states it, quietly, and lets it hang there in the air."
"And who are you, Sir, curtain-material-wise?"

I looked at him. Or, rather, through him, to the far off place where the truth lies concealed beneath the evergreen bush of indifference, assumptions, distraction, and the fear that nothing will ever come to any good. I looked beneath this bush, noted what I saw, and said:
"I'm a velvet person."
"Velvet, Sir. Any particular velvet?"
"Crushed velvet. Crushed, but not ultimately defeated. Do you have a velvet that's lost a lot of battles but still has a fighting chance in the war?"
"I believe we may have such a velvet, Sir. What colour?"

"What colour? I don't know, but whatever colour, I'd like a shade that's poised between light and dark, that's neither dull nor bright. I'd like a hue that says hold me, but don't fence me in. A tone that says touch me, but respect my right to pull away, perhaps even to shudder. Do you have such a colour?"

"I believe so. Any particular pattern?"

"Yes, I'd like a pattern, but I'd like a patternless pattern, if you get my meaning."

"Very good."

"I want a pattern that says: Here is someone who's taken a good look. Who's looked at life, held it up to the light and said, 'I see.' Who's looked into the dark corners of their own soul, held the gaze of what looked back at them, and said, 'That's me.'"

And the assistant said: "I'll just see if I have that in stock then, Sir."

I said: "Thanks."

He came back a couple of minutes later, with a roll of cloth.

"Is that it?"

"I'm afraid not, Sir. We didn't have any crushed-but-not-defeated velvet with a neither/nor colour and patternless pattern which implies someone who's had a good, hard look in stock, Sir."

"Oh."

"I'm afraid we sold the last few metres yesterday. To someone from Social Services."

"Oh."

"But we do have this pale beige."

"Yes? What would it say about me?"

"It would say: 'Here is someone who knew a bargain when he saw one at £2.99 a metre. And wasn't afraid to have people think he was a pillock.'"

I said "Fine, I'll take that one."

LOW KEY

I'm low-key, me
I'm a low-key bloke, see
I do a bit of DIY
I'm a member of the RAC

I'm a low-key bloke – but I'm not blokey
I like a joke – but I'm not jokey
I'm too low-key for that

Okay, occasionally
I'll push the boat out
And at our local social club night
I like to sing like Kylie

And up there in my highly
Thought-of karaoke croak
I'll sing: I should be so low-key
Low-key low-key low-key

I do my shopping locally
And when I buy my vegetables
I buy them by the ki
Lo, kilo kilo ki(lo)

If the going gets tough I can handle myself
I do low Ki Aikido
I used to do Tai Chi
But it was too demonstrative for me

I'm undemonstrative, me. Why?
Because I like to keep my under-monster
Under lock and key. See?
I'm low-key, me

Once tense is tense
Twice tense is too tense
Three tense is quite stressed
Four tense is fraught
Five tense is frightening
Six tense is tightening
Seven tense is distressed
Eight tense is taut
Nine tense is intense
Ten tense is uptight
Eleven tense – keep your distance
Twelve tense just might…
Thirteen tense – RIGHT! THAT'S IT! I've had it up to here
with your tense times table, it's not a proper poem it's not a
proper times table and that's the last time you make me
make a fool of myself in public… (continue ranting
indefinitely, then fade, and look sheepish)

All right, okay, I own up, I am frightened
of spiders, earwigs, moths, crane-flies and bees.
My bowels loosen up, my sphincter's tightened,
there's always a slight tremor about my knees
when these creatures encroach on my environs.
And when they run or brush against my skin
I make a sound like old-style air-raid sirens.
I'm not proud of the state I can get in.
But I don't choose to flinch, it's a compulsion
which I am dealing with as best I can.
And overcoming such a strong revulsion
is practically a life's work for a man.
But when I feel more comfortable with insects
I'll see if I can't start to relax a bit more around people.

I worried that my thoughts would show
And everyone would look and see
And not just look and see but know
The depths of my depravity

I worried that my shares would drop
And ill winds fill my patched-up sail
I worried that if I should stop
My worrying the crops would fail

I worried that the passing years
Would prove too short – or far too long
And yet, in spite of all these fears
Things nonetheless went badly wrong

BILLY HAS BEAUTIFUL URGES

Billy has beautiful urges
They're quite like yours and mine
Just that little bit more beautiful
Deeply felt and fine
Yes Billy has beautiful urges
From time to time

Billy had a girlfriend
And while they made love
Billy would whisper beautiful things into her ear
– quotes from Ram Dass, The Road Less Travelled
and Love Is Letting Go Of Fear –
And when they'd finish Billy would roll over, exhausted
And his girlfriend would go Hmm, that was lovely, Billy
Then she'd go into the bathroom
And take out her earplugs
     Billy has beautiful urges
     But he doesn't have a girlfriend any more

Billy went into a Butcher's Shop
And tried to heal a joint of meat
Through the laying on of hands
But the butcher didn't understand
He threw Billy out into the street
Saying: I'll give you laying on of hands!
And Billy said: That's beautiful – we could do an exchange!
     Billy has beautiful urges
     But people find Billy strange

Billy tried to forge a much-needed link with authority
By rubbing tea-tree oil on a police-dog handler
Who seemed to have a bit of a skin infection
But the police-dog handler's police dog got the wrong impression
He tried to give his handler police protection
And afterwards the police-dog handler and his dog
Had to have one month's compassionate leave
And Billy had to have a tetanus injection
    Billy has beautiful urges
    But he experiences a lot of rejection

Billy is too beautiful to harbour feelings of anger, resentment
Or the desire to hurt or maim
Such feelings can find no purchase
In Billy's beautiful frame
Instead they camp in the suburbs of Billy's aura
In a grey-black cloud which hovers always near
Whispering seductive suggestions in Billy's oh-so-
                                      impressionable ear

There's currently an urge building up in Billy
To hold his favourite auntie's head underwater
Just long enough for her soul to leave her body
And go off and become a fairy –
    Yes Billy has beautiful urges
    And it's very, very scary

You think you know someone. Perhaps you do.
But can you ever know a person, really?
Take my friend Jane. Here is a case in point.
I really thought I knew my old friend Jane.
I'd go round to her house, and she to mine.
We had the key to one another's door.
We disagreed sometimes, but got on fine –
We had what I would call a real rapport.
I felt Jane was a friend I could rely on.
But all along she was a man called Brian.

When they made you they did things differently.
They focused less on outer measurement
but sensed instead what inner treasure meant.
Putting aside pinpoint accuracy
they drew freehand without consulting charts.
Breaking with precedent, re-writing rules
they set to work with wooden-handled tools
and wandered down forbidden lanes for parts.
Amazing what you pick up 'nearly new' –
yet something in you's timeless, musty, old...
You like things simple, unspectacular,
organic, natural. When they made you
it wasn't so much that they broke the mould –
more that they scraped it off you with a spatula.

WHAT ARE YOU?

You're a dream debutante, gene databank, love bucket, pocket
primate, utterly crackpot smacked not lottery jackpot

What are you?

You're a wide-eyed windfall, a button-pushing pinball

Life-altering all-terrain boogie buggy passenger – you're a
huggy cuddle craver, you're a snugly cradle raver – you're a
bit of a groover, a duvet remover, embedded bed-jewel,
schedule re-arranger, stranger softener, smile widener,
shoulder-broadener extraordinaire

You're a suckler for nourishment, a chuckler, a cackler, you're
a tackle tinkerer, you're a rugby tackler. Quick thinker, deep
stinker, aromatherapist

You're a home improvement, a luminous ruminant, a whole
new artistic movement, not-always-the-gentlest
experimentalist, nipple twister, blister-burster

Cup breaker, beaker leaker, laughter lover, sensation seeker,
you're a much sought after after dinner gobbledegook speaker
(Aren't you?)

You're a VIP doing VI poo, dream-snatcher, germ-catcher,
charming squirmer, worm-harmer, goody grabber, crab walker,
eye-jabber, Daddy stalker

You're an up-chucker, flannel sucker, mucker upper, upper-
body workout kit, shit manufacturer, bachelor botherer,
authority ignorer, brain re-wirer, furniture restorer requirer

You're crap-happy when you're out and about, you're the
opposite of fossil, you're a bustle sprout

Indiscriminate techno lover, take-no-prisoners soft toy
smotherer, brother annoyer, book-about-raising-boys destroyer

Yes you are – you're a dream debutante, gene databank, love
bucket, pocket primate, utterly crackpot smacked not
lottery jackpot

What are you?

No. 37 My Uncle Hamish

Overnight my Uncle Hamish
found the Lord
and became an Amish.

Now he rises at five
(to tend his allotment)
and feels more alive.

As he shuns all the trappings of modern life
(apart from his up-to-the-minute Scandinavian wife
                              which is nice)
all the mysteries of the Universe are gradually unfurled.

His only vice
is occasionally listening to Gardener's World.

No. 62 My Uncle Norman

It shocked us all when my Uncle Norman
saw the light* and became a Mormon.
He packed his sponge-bag, leapt on his scooter,
said: "Cheery-bye, I'm off to Utah.
I'll probably be gone a while."

He had a strange seraphic smile
playing about his face.
As if he came from outer space.
Which he might well have done.

*or at least *a* light

A few inches above the skirting-board
it sits. A socket. Ready for a plug
to be inserted. Which will have a cord
that stretches to the heater on the rug.
Look. Three accommodating oblong holes.
The top one longer than the other two.
One in. One out. One earth. Their humble goal's
to let the electricity come through.
Three holes. A small domestic Trinity.
Three aspects of the power that is the Source.
Which may be likened to Divinity.
Which in those Star Wars films was called The Force.
    In this material world how very odd
    to find a socket leads us back to God.

SOMEONE SOMEWHERE

In times of food and plenty
In times of fear and doubt
When all my plates are empty
When all my stars are out

On nights of average rainfall
On days of standard sun
When breathing in is painful
When I feel I've not begun

Still some things must be sacred
And someone must be blessed
I love you when you're naked
I love you when you're dressed

In times of void and plenty
In times of void and drought
When outside I am empty
When inside I am out

I lie beside you naked
I walk beside you dressed
And some things still are sacred
And someone, somewhere, blessed

My first floor flat is directly opposite a vegetarian
restaurant, Willow, which serves fine food all year round.
What follows is a true story and happened just the other day.

I was walking past Willow up to the Post Office. I glanced in
and there by the window table I saw two men, hugging. They
were both swarthy, with thick, dark designer stubble on
cheek and neck. One had a ponytail. One had a beret lying
beside him on the table like a floppy dog-bowl. Both wore
colourful baggy trousers. I thought: Hmmm, two men having
a hug. Then I carried on to the Post Office.

I did my business at the Post Office and came back the same
way. They were still there – clasped together, eyes closed. I
thought: Hmmm, long hug. And I carried on down to the
bank. I was a good ten minutes at the bank, then I wandered
back up town. In the window of Willow the two men were
still hugging. They hadn't moved. I began to feel a bit
uncomfortable. I thought: What's going on here? Was one of
them deeply upset, or both of them? Were both of them
afraid to break the hug for fear of seeming to have a fear of
intimacy? Could it be a sponsored hug for charity? There was
no way of knowing, so I went upstairs to my flat.

I pottered about a bit, watered the plants, did a bit of Tai
Chi, a bit of ty-ping, and tried not to think about the hug.
But a glance out of the window saw them still there. Same
men. Same hug. I can't explain it, but hysteria began to well
up in me. I began to panic. I didn't know what to do, so I
phoned my friend, Chris.

I said: "Chris, there are two men in the window of Willow
restaurant, hugging." He said: "So?" I said: "They're swarthy,
they're wearing colourful baggy trousers, one of them's got a
ponytail." He said: "So?" I said: "They've been there for over
twenty-five minutes." He said: "Hmmm." I said: "I don't know

what to do Chris, it's been over twenty-five minutes since I first saw them." "I see." "What am I going to do Chris?" He said: "Matt," I said: "Chris," he said: "Matt, it's their hug." "It's their hug," "But it's your fear." "My fear." He said: "Face your fear, Matt." "How, Chris?" "Move towards it. I want you to go down to Willow and face your fear. You can do it." I said: "Thanks Chris, I can do it." And I did.

I went down to Willow to face my fear and discovered I wasn't the only one affected by the hug. Some people were dropping ten p's and other coins into the beret as they went by, treating it as a form of indoor busking. Others were making complaints: "We're not happy with the hug in the window. This is a vegetarian restaurant and it's a very meaty hug. We're not comfortable." But the management were firm that their policy was to support same-sex hugs with no time limit – and if customers weren't happy with men hugging perhaps they shouldn't be in a vegetarian restaurant in Totnes in the first place. Others disconcerted by the hug had formed a small self-help group in a room at the back, so I joined them.

We sat in a circle and shared feelings that the hug was bringing up. I spoke frankly of my fear and felt accepted by the group. Another man shared how hard it was for him because his father had only ever shown affection to him when they were underwater. He was having breathing difficulties. I thought: this is valuable and instructive, but has anyone asked the huggers how they feel? For my fear was giving way to curiosity and I had an urgent desire to know what was going on for the two huggers.

Rolling all my courage into a ball I approached them, coughed sensitively, and asked: "Excuse me. Is everything OK?" The one with the ponytail opened his eyes. They met mine. I saw in them relief, gratitude, exhaustion. His mouth moved and I lip-read, rather than heard, the word "Help". An urgent, whispered exchange followed, and all became apparent: They had become stuck together, but not for charity, or fear of showing fear of intimacy. An ordinary embrace had gone horribly wrong: Their hug was so snug, their stubble so dense, the follicle spacing ratios on their faces so exactly matched, they had become velcro'd together. We couldn't separate them immediately, or one of them would have lost face. Instead, using a pipette filled with olive oil we drizzled drops down between them, letting the seeping oil soften the tangled fuzz, then gently, tenderly, prised them apart. It was a poignant moment.

For me the whole experience was profoundly moving. I had faced a fear whose source remains mysterious, I had shared my pain with strangers and I had asked in my own way the burning question, "What ails thee?" – not of a wounded king but of two fellow knights-errant. And there was more to come. As I wandered home in a grateful, heightened state, I was vouchsafed on the way an awesome vision of Araldite, god of male bonding.

MAXIM FOR THE TROOPS

We're only human
after all
and even a
Colonel of Truth
sometimes
needs a Soldier
to cry on

I wasn't always this brash, Northern extrovert who murmurs so assertively into the microphone. In fact I was a very shy, withdrawn, child. Acutely so. And like many shy, withdrawn children I had an imaginary friend. The trouble was my imaginary friend was also very shy and withdrawn. Technically he was autistic. And he wouldn't have anything to do with me. It was very difficult. Interestingly, being shy and withdrawn in his own right he had an imaginary friend of his own, and the two of them used to play together and exclude me. Kids of that age can be really cruel, can't they?

There's a happy ending to all this though, because a couple of years ago my imaginary friend got in touch with me. Completely out of the blue I had an imaginary letter from him. I replied to it, he wrote again, and in no time he'd become my imaginary pen-pal. Like many pen-pals the world over we did an exchange. First of all he came to live with me for a while in the real world, which he found really challenging. Then I went to stay with him in his imaginary world. I loved it. I loved it so much, in fact, that I'm still here...

On a visit to Buckfastleigh Butterfly Farm and Otter
Sanctuary I read on a poster that when the caterpillar pupates
inside the chrysalis it breaks down into a liquid state, into
soup, before metamorphosing into a butterfly – which is, it
said, a universal symbol for psychological wholeness.

I thought: you can't stay a caterpillar for ever
        Not even if you're a caterpillar of the community
I thought: you've not yet passed your metamorphose-by-date
        It's time to move on. It's time to pupate

And so I wove myself a self-catering chrysalis
A protective outer casing
Composed, in my case
Of fixed habits, stock phrases, trademark mannerisms
And an easy-automatic affability –
And prepared for pupation, mutation
Emotional promotion

After a while I wondered why
Instead of firming and toning and turning
Into a wholesome butterfly
I began to disband, to droop, to liquify, turn to soup

I went into a crisis in my chrysalis, I looked around
But found no emergency cord to pull
No glass to break or antidote to take
You can't halt the progress of metamorphosis
Not when it's a metaphor for a deep core process

It is the norm
Among those who would transform
To experience temporary loss of form
Before they can regroup
Your ingredients must revert to soup

You must submit, surrender your solidity
There's no biological or legal loophole
You go out of your salad days into the soup-bowl
Helpless as when you arrived in the cradle
You're up soup creek – without a ladle
     You're pupa-soup

And though there's little cachet or social status
In being a little sachet of oceanic stardust
On the side of your pupa-soup packet you can honestly say:
Nothing added, nothing taken away

In our case of course we become alphabet soup
Our cells are letters encrypted in code
Interred in an unpronounceable word –
And as our constitution is re-written
We become a variation on a theme
A re-interpretation of a half-remembered dream –
But I trust as I recover a sense of who I am
There shall emerge a singing cabalistic anagram
     A poet in translation
     With the inescapable sensation
That here, at the intersection at the top of the spine
Here where antennae and two wings converge
     Shall be words
Glistening wet with the primal soup slime:

In the beginning
     meets
          Dearly beloved
     meets
Once upon a time

No. 46   My Uncle Ken

When my Uncle Ken
was born
he liked it so much that later in life
he decided to do it again.
So he became a Born-Again Christian.
Not satisfied with that he became
a born again and again and again and again
Buddhist.
He's already impatient
for his next incarnation.

No. 216   My Aunt Matilda

When my Aunt Matilda
told us she was going to become a builder
we laughed
and said "Don't be daft."

But while we scoffed
she converted her loft.

The shed door's busted
It has a screw loose
How do you do
I am that loose screw
I've eroded and rusted
I'm beginning to slip
I can't be trusted
To keep my grip
I've kept my head
But lost my thread
And I don't mean to whinge
But when your sole purpose in life
Is to hold a hinge
In place
– To stay still in a space
So that others might swing –
And you fail
You feel beyond the pale
You might as well be a common nail
I was brought up to believe
That tight is right
That to bite into the wood is good
That a sound screw should
Be both at one and at war
With the wood, admit no truce
But sit snug as or snugger than a steel papoose
Better dead than lose your thread
But what's a screw to do?
It's hard to stay fixed
When you're broken
And my poor shed door it
Hangs there disjointed, disappointed
While I, though a little bitter
Am a slightly better metaphor for it

I walked with my Hypothesis
across the stony plain
we followed my pale proboscis
both out and back again
      just my Hypothesis and I
      beneath a chalky, crimson sky

we wandered cracked and cosy tracks
in states of dry elation
both suffered mild and brief attacks
of hyperventilation
      and all the world to me seemed fine
      for my Hypothesis was mine

it seemed no earthly force could mar
or break what lay between us
we travelled true, we travelled far
two starry-eyed believers
      and all I knew back then was this:
      I loved my dear Hypothesis

I loved that theory, loved it more
than emeralds or rubies
and did not see step through the door
the puffed-up shape of Hubris
      did I not know (and know I knew)
      that my Hypothesis was true?

in Hubris' wake there walked, concealed
its ruthless ally Nemesis
who in a flash of truth revealed:
Your love has shaky premises
      how could you be so blind to miss
      the flaw in your Hypothesis?

I heard its voice, I heard it speak
it sowed a poison seed of doubt
saying: Your Hypothesis is weak
what do you think you're on about?
        my model of the Universe
        began to seem a bit perverse

for when I looked I had been blind
I glanced beneath and quickly found
the edifice I had in mind
was built on non-existent ground
        I'd made that model with my brain
        and now I'd have to start again

so play that slow, funereal waltz
and let the woodwind moan
for my Hypothesis proved false
and I am left alone
        I never shall regain the bliss
        I knew with my Hypothesis

my love was tender, young and fresh
and passionate – it could be said
if my Hypothesis had flesh
I would have taken it to bed
        and made love with it all night long
        let no-one say such things are wrong

since my Hypothesis collapsed
(as man-made structures tend to do)
I feel sufficient time's elapsed
for me to take the longer view
        and say, now that my sight is clear:
        Oh well – it was a nice idea

THEY SAY THAT FISH

They say that fish don't have a word for water
The same way birds don't have a word for air
That bricks, quite rightly, have no word for mortar
And angels, bless them, have no word for prayer

Most bees, when questioned, have no word for honey
The Oedipal don't have a word for Freud
The stinking rich don't need to carry money
The non-existent have no word for void

Though it may take us aeons to achieve it
– Perhaps just to conceive of it's enough
It's an effort, frankly, just to half-believe it –
Our world may one day have no word for love

IF LOVE

If love
can build a bridge,
can affection
put up a shelf?

And the lonely hearts clutch their lonely parts
They know you can't make honey without gathering pollen
They're practising in private to perfect their lonely arts
Run their fingers up and down the lonely hearts column
(and it says:)

Former coal-miner needs to make a fresh start
Seeks a slow-burning woman with a solid-fuel heart

Off-season naturist with all-over tan
Requires positive, outgoing, weatherproof man

Chubby-cheeked cherub with a cheeky-chap smile
Seeks a soft-centred seraph to lead down the aisle

Down-hearted of Suffolk seeks Norfolk broad
Lady with life-raft sought by man overboard

Saucy seductress, can ring her own bell
Seeks soft-touch celebrity to kiss and tell

Brass-necked from Barnsley, can blow his own trumpet
Wants traditional, old-fashioned, hot-buttered crumpet

Distressed damsel with Rapunzel locks
Seeks bright white knight with own suggestion box

Freshwater fisherman wants worm on a hook
Man-hungry midget seeks short-order cook

Hardware store owner with colourful past
Wants to give his love freely (while stocks last)

Threadbare widow without a stitch underneath
Seeks gentleman, fifties, must have own teeth

Speakeasy waitress with ball-bearing hips
Seeks deaf and dumb waiter to read her lips

Bristly Scots thistle seeks English rose
Cat with no scent seeks a dog with no nose

Uninsured man (feels a bit insecure)
Seeks a guaranteed girl he can fix to the floor

Librarian for whom love is long overdue
Wants a love of his own on a table for two

Wolf in sheep's clothing whose ardour is cooling
Hunts red-blooded woman for mutual drooling

Southern belle hankers for hunky hillbilly
Saddle-sore stallion seeks unfussy filly

Muscle-bound builder with high-rise ambition
Aches for angelic architect with planning permission

Crotchetty granny with hand-knitted sulk
Wants to give someone orders to buy things in bulk

Life gets so lonely amongst the pots and the pans
So dishwater woman seeks rubber-glove man

Woman on heat sought by man in a rut
Chain-smoking woman seeks smouldering butt

Dyslexic debutante seeks illegible earl
Optical illusion looks for gullible girl

LONely Hearts SONG

Fastidious feline with retractable claws
Requires manicured man with a Steve McQueen jaw

Philosophy professor, never been kissed's
In need of literal lady to prove he exists

Tattooed woman with a bird on each breast
Seeks a high-flying husband to feather her nest

Vietnamese vets look for Siamese twins
Guilty-as-charged seek forgiveness of sins

Vulnerable Venus needs man to protect her
Toyboy available. (Batteries extra)

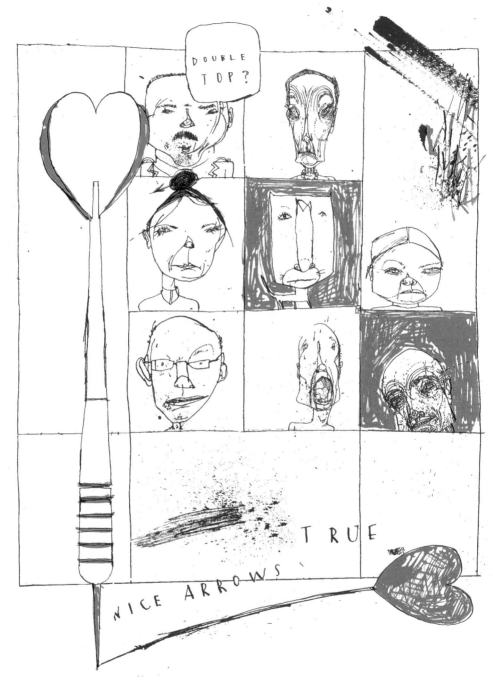

And the lonely hearts clutch their lonely parts
They know you can't make honey without gathering pollen
They're practising in private to perfect their lonely arts
Run their fingers up and down the lonely hearts column

I was told Susamasamoona *is a special greeting reserved for the time of the full moon. In fact it's not.*

At the time of the full moon I said to my sister, on the landing
    Susamasamoona, O sister, Susamasamoona
And we bowed, and she smiled, and said the same to me

At the time of the waxing half moon I said to my brother
                           on the stairs
    Masamoonasusa, O brother, Masamoonasusa
And he laughed, lightly, and we shook hands

At the time of the waning half moon I said to my mother
                        outside the kitchen
    Moonasusamasa, O mother, Moonasusamasa
And she nodded, patiently, and brushed some egg from my cheek

At the time of moon dark I mouthed silently to my father
                        by the tool shed
    Oonasusamasam, O father, Oonasusamasam
And he sighed, wearily, and said: "When are you going to get
                        a job?"

When you can leave
        and yet remain
Go quite, quite mad
        and yet stay sane
When you can stay
        and yet be gone
When you have lost
        and also won
When you are true
        and also false
When you are you
        yet someone else...

When you can come
        yet not be called
Can comb your hair
        and yet be bald
When you can scratch
        and yet not itch
When you are poor
        yet stinking rich
When you can shift
        and yet not budge
Can wear a wig
        and yet not judge...

When you've attained
    this blessed state
Are both the garden
    and the gate
Are both the gander
    and the goose
Are constipated
    and yet loose
When you can fail
    and yet succeed
Be self-sufficient
    yet feel need...

When you have mastered
    all these things
Can be a bird
    yet have no wings
When you can live
    and yet be dead
There's no point get-
    -ting out of bed...

I washed myself today with seal-shaped soap
Fresh from the Body Shop
I shine with a Body Shop seal-shaped soap-induced sheen
The reason for the seal-shaped soap
On the Body Shop shelves
Is to help us, lightly soiled consumers, ourselves
Make a fuss about the raw deal the seal is getting
It's an appeal for us to feel for the seal
To get into a lather on the seal's behalf
And raise such a stink
We help save it from becoming extinct

But while my feelings for the seal
Are as soft and tender as my skin
When I've washed in Body Shop seal-shaped soap
I don't hold out too much hope
For the seal-shaped soap
Doing much to help
The real seal-shaped seal
Escape the raw deal we've handed it
And I ask myself: Would the Body Shop seal-shaped soap
Get the real seal-shaped seal's seal of approval?

Short-term I can't help but feel
The real seal's fondest and deepest wish
Would be for someone, somewhere
To throw it a fish

I caught the sun today
But you should have seen the star
That got away

Go on, strike a match
Break open the Bryant and May
Strike gently and away from body
Then listen to what I say

Though it says on the side I'm a safety match
Don't be misled
Once you release the genie of the matchbox
I have to be fed

I'll always come
When you click your flint fingers
Call me up out of the latent
Into the literal –
A tiny tongue to curl around your kindling
To sip the thin gruel of your gas
Snuggle round the ring at your selected setting

But if you think there's such a thing
As a tame flame – think again

Once out of harness
I go feral
Become furnace

For I am the tongue that seeks to taste
Far more than what is on my plate
The tongue that's never satisfied
That just wants more, and wants it fried

I am the tongue that phrases things differently:
        You say, Kindling – I say, Hors d'oeuvres
        You say, Furniture – I say, Next course
        You say, Oh God Call 999 – I say, Hey! This is brilliant!

One little scratch, my head will catch
And you have 20 seconds of contained potential
A biddable flicker
To light your blue touch paper
Dance naked on your birthday cake

But before you blow me out
And make your wish, answer this:
     Do you feel lucky?

Go on, strike a match
Break open the Bryant and May
     Go ahead.
     Make my day

Whenever Jessica made a slip
Her father would say to her
        Jess! Get a grip!
If ever she burped or slurped her tea
        He'd say: Jessica, sip!
        That's my girl. Get a grip
And when she succumbed to the urge to skip
Or let rip with a fart
Or to say something smart...
        Jessica! Get a grip!
And if she came back with a quick, clever quip
He'd hiss: Less of your lip, Jess
And fetch her a clip
Round the ear
And if Jessica let slip a tear
It was: Jess, wipe your face
That's my girl. Get a grip
And if she woke him up from an afternoon kip
        Then he'd practically flip:
        JESSICA! Get... a... grip

Eventually Jessica had such a firm grip
        She was completely rigid
        And had to be put on a drip
And her father (bless him)
Would make the twenty-mile
        Round trip
        To her bedside, and say
Come on Jessie – give us a smile!

They also serve
Who only
Serve themselves

You are
    A four-cornered star, shining rustily in hot water
You are
    The perforated parachute that makes my morning
    Landings soft when I crash in from dreamland

You are a savoury scented sandbag
    As half-empty as it is half-full
    Your permeable membrane an inverted flood-wall

You're the force that through infusion drives my waking hour
    A freshwater sponge, soaking up my power
    To resist you, I insist you're always welcome to
                        muddy my waters

    For when I'm blue I brew you up
    And pour you out into my cup
    And offered as soothing ointment to my oesophagus
    You are not a disappointment

    Although you are (a disappointment) as a
                        Christmas decoration
    And also as a duvet you've a very low tog-rating

    Produce of more than one country
    You are an intercontinental holistic missile
    Yes I'll always keep our mid-morning appointment
    For the best of many heavens is
    Elevenses
    And when you're hot for me
    To be honest
    Just one is
    Enough per pot for me

Consolation prize, foul-weather friend
Treasure at the rainbow's end
Calm-inducer, tongue-loosener
Rescue-remedy, biscuit softener
You're often a subtle social worker
Or community relations officer

Peace-broker, mediator
China-stainer, radiator
Nerve-soother, mood-changer
Don't you *ever* be a stranger

My multi-tasking flask-filler
          Waker-upper
          Cuppa-maker
          Throat-stroker

          I'll see you later…

TO A VERY SPECIAL SLOPE

You're such a radiant gradient
A smooth one, not a hilly one
Your red-rimmed sign says you're one in nine
But to me you're one in a million

There's something I can almost touch
        (And not to would be such a waste)
I try – perhaps I try too much
        There's something I can almost taste

There's someone – but they're very shy
        And far away inside their shell
And yet I don't know how or why
        There's something I can almost smell

There's something, I am positive
        Just out of sight but very clear
I'm sure it was – or was it? – if
        We sit quite still it might come near

And some time – if we're very good
        And only step between the cracks
We may stand where that something stood
        And quiver in our anoraks

And even if we're very bad
        And make it worse by getting caught
There's something almost very sad
        That's neither feeling quite nor thought

And though it may not leave a trace
        Or show up on our instruments
We'll know we've almost seen its face
        And felt its subtle influence

We'll know, though it cannot be proved
        That something nearly not quite there
Has touched our mind's membrane and moved
        Absurdly small amounts of air

CIRCULAR SONNET

Does absence really make the heart grow fonder
or does it simply let the mind forget?
(The mind's a fishing vessel, prone to wander,
and absent friends can slip clean through its net.)
I know I do not think of you that often –
just once or twice a month I'd say, if that.
But when I do I feel my heart part soften
and pretty soon I'm purring (like a cat).
My instinct's to sit down and write a letter
but when I do the words come out all wrong.
Perhaps a simple phone-call would be better
or possibly a poem or a song.
And so I wrote this sonnet just for you:
though I'm not sure, yet, who I'll send it to.

Sleep on then, love, I will not wake you, though
it's lonely keeping vigil at your side.
A part of me would like to have you know
that I am here. Awake. Alert. But pride
forbids my acting from this loneliness,
both pride and a respect for where you are:
a world whose landscape I can only guess –
as far away from me as any star
whose pinpoint pricks the conscience of the night.
My crumpled scruples cavil at the thought
of waking you. It wouldn't be quite right.
So here with you, alone, so oddly caught
between two distances, I sit and sigh.
And hum, a bit too loud, a lullaby.

Part of me is punctual – it turns up right on time
Part of me is functional – though slightly past its prime
Part of me is criminal – it's quite against the law
And part of me's subliminal – and kind of either/or
Part of me is lowly – it lows just like a cow
Part of me is holy – at least holier-than-thou
Part of me is actually more solid than it seems
And part of me is factual
      But most of me is dreams

Part of me is truculent – don't look that way at me
Part of me is succulent – suck it and you'll see
Part of me's detestable – or so people have said
And part of me's suggestible – or so people have said
Part of me's competitive – it only wants to win
And part of me's repetitive – or so people have said
Part of me's interminable – it goes on and on and on
And on and on and on and on and on and on (and on)
This part of me's prolific – it writes reams and reams and reams
And part of me's terrific
      But most of me is dreams

Parts of me are distant – and yet can seem so near
Parts of me are whispers – which the other parts can't hear
Parts of me are broken – and tremble to the touch
And these parts can be spoken – but I don't speak them much
Part of me is pensive – I think. But I don't know.
Part of me's defensive – ... ... *so*?
Part of me's celestial – it gleams and beams and gleams
And part of me is bestial (*grrrrrr*)
      But most of me is dreams

Part of me is tiny – but not the part you think
Part of me is shiny – and a pleasing shade of pink
Part of me is laudable – it's for a worthy cause
And part of me's inaudible – (like imaginary gorse*)

mouthed silently

Part of me is hairy – to be honest not a lot
Part of me's contrary – no it's not
Part of me's co-operative – it plays so well in teams
And part of me's inoperative
      But most of me is dreams

Parts of me are latent – lurking dormant underneath
Parts of me are blatant – for some reason they're called Keith
Parts of me have stamina – because I do Chi Gung
And part of me's my anima – according to the psychology of
      Carl Gustav Jung
Part of me is piddling – yet full of cosmic yearning
And part of me is fiddling – while the rest of me is burning
Part of me is fluent – it flows as sure as streams
While part of me plays truant
      But most of me – as I've tried to emphasise here – is dreams

Are you a plant that needs to be re-potted?
Are you a fern without a special frond?
Are you some string that needs to be unknotted?
Are you some magic looking for a wand?

Are you twice shy because you've been once bitten?
Are you a tyre that needs to be re-trod?
Are you a verse that needs to be re-written?
Are you so PC your path through life's all Plod?

Do your past glories need to be recycled?
Or are you a dog who's yet to have his day?
Are you a line that needs to be St. Michaeled?
Did you get your genes from Man at D'N'A?*

Are you a joke that needs an explanation?
Or are you a secret far too dark to tell?
Are you a star without a constellation?
Are you a wish that's locked inside a well?

Because I'm an experienced workshop facilitator who
        specialises in freeing up human predicaments with
        poignantly accurate metaphor
I believe metaphor is literally a sort of special kind of
        magic key
And having your situation encapsulated in a single
        illuminating image is something you'll feel so much
        the better for
Plus it means I can make a tidy living running therapeutic
        imaging workshops with twelve to fifteen people
        paying £220 a head and live here in beautiful
        South Devon, handy for rugged Dartmoor and the
        spirit-revitalising sea

*great line

No. 26   Ned

While recuperating in bed
having been struck on the head
by a falling prism,
my good friend Ned
became unduly interested
in Mithraism.
Fortunately he never fully recovered consciousness.

No. 12   Me In My Younger Days

Early in my mis-spelt yough
I wondered if it would be a good idea
to become a Moonie.
Or not.
My sister, bless her,
asked me what in God's name I was up to,
and had I become a complete and utter loony?
Or what?
The thing of it is, I told her,
I feel the need for some spiritual succour.
Then she was kind enough to take me aside
and point out the subtle difference
between receiving spiritual succour
and simply being one.

Mother, there are some Bandaged Alaskans at the door.

What do they want?

They're collecting.

There's some loose change in my purse, dear.

They say they don't want loose change, they want lasting change with peace, justice and bandages for all. They want to come in and engage in meaningful dialectic on the sofa.

Tell them not now dear, Mrs. Brinscombe's due any minute.

Mother?

Yes dear?

The Bandaged Alaskans have taken both me and Mrs. Brinscombe hostage, and they're going to hold us in testing conditions in the front garden unless you accede to their demands.

We never accede to the demands of terrorists, dear. It only encourages them.

Mother?

Yes dear?

I want you to know that I have become a Bandaged Alaskan. Their goals are my goals. Their demands are my demands. We are no longer separately willed entities.

Oh dear. You've allowed yourself to be brainwashed and turned against your own. Typical.

Not at all. I've been awakened to the fact that *previously* I'd been brainwashed to the point where I didn't even *recognise* my own.

Don't be silly.

I'm not being silly.

You're a silly, ungrateful boy, just like your father, and there won't be any supper for you tonight.

I don't need any supper tonight. I've never felt so alive, so myself, so new yet part of an ancient continuity, so transparent yet opaque, so committed yet irresponsible. So *free*.

Huh. Free?

Yes, free. I never knew freedom could come from giving up all you once held dear, all that gave life meaning and security, to commit yourself to an ill-defined struggle with a group whose aims are unclear, whose methods are unsound, whose leaders are incoherent, and whose bodies are wrapped in layers of unnecessary bandages.

Hmph. What about Mrs. Brinscombe?

What *about* Mrs. Brinscombe?

How does Mrs. Brinscombe feel about all this?

Mrs. Brinscombe is an acrylic-coated reactionary. She prefers to cling to the rotten corpse of what has been and refuses to give suck to the squalling, puking, nappy-filling aliveness of what is, what shall be, what has to be.

Ha. Mrs. Brinscombe is made of sterner stuff! Anyway. What are your demands?

We demand the right to make demands. We politely request the right to make requests; and we insist absolutely on our right to absolutely insist on things.

And?

We also demand fresh bandages for all our limbs, whether or not our wounds are actual or metaphorical. We demand the right to be appreciated and commended for what we are, rather than disapproved of and condemned because of what we did recently.

Is that all?

We'd also like some anti-septic cream, a puncture repair kit and some aloe vera.

[Sound of police siren: *ner-ner, ner-ner*]

Uh-oh! It's the police! Quick!

Thank goodness you arrived, Officer, they'd turned my own son against me and God only knows what they'd have done to Mrs. Brinscombe.

Fortunately Mrs. Brinscombe is unscathed and we have returned your son to you, the brainwashing has worn off.

Did you capture any alive?

Neither alive nor dead Ma'am. I'm afraid the Bandaged Alaskans slipped out of their bandages and successfully blended in with mainstream society. Their sort are always difficult to spot and more difficult still to weed out.

Still, at least I have my son back, don't I?

In a sense. But though I no longer espouse the cause of the Bandaged Alaskans – who I can see now are nothing more than fetishistic origami figurines – I feel changed. I will never again be the same person.

Why not? Mrs. Brinscombe hasn't changed.

Who can say. I only know that having once looked at the world, however misguidedly, from behind unnecessary bandages, I can never return to the life I once knew. A part of me will always shiver in the presence of hypocrisy and injustice. And I will always wear an elostoplast somewhere about my person to remind me that once I stood tall and made a stand, if only for a few minutes and in my own front garden. It's hard to see the son you knew ever returning.

Would it help if we gave you guitar lessons?

And a mountain bike?

And a mountain bike. Do you feel more yourself now?

I feel strangely ambivalent, but it's as close as I think I'll get.

It'll have to do, then.

Yes.

Well, let's hope we all live happily ever after.

Yes, let's.

VIOLENCE POEM

I went up to a yobhead
and I looked him in the eye
and I said, "Hi."
And he said, "Yeah? Yeah?"
And I said, "Why
are you so violent?"

Well he shrugged a little shrug,
and he sighed a little sigh,
and he kicked me in the testicles
and gave me this reply:

"It may be hard to credit
 but I'm just a little shy."

"I see," I said. "The 't' is silent."

Then I ran.

Postscript:
Strangely enough I happened to be going the same way a
couple of weeks later and I ran in to him again at the exact
same place. He hadn't moved. Seeing me, a confused, hurt
expression appeared on his face. "Oi," he said, "are you
calling me a violin?"

REVENGE OF THE POET

I'll write a poem
That'll show'em

Your face is like the back end of a bus.
No, do not take offence, for none is meant.
It is intended as a compliment.
If you would just calm down and hush your fuss
I'll tell you, if I can, just how the view
of that rear end of bus as it pulls out
from the bus-stop or rounds a roundabout
can fill my throbbing head with thoughts of you:
  Yours is the face that I've been waiting for,
  but when I try to reach you you've just been
  and gone. I'd travel, if I could afford it,
  to your sweet terminus, I'd pay that fare,
  yet you elude me still –
         see what I mean?
  Plus: you have advertising on your forehead.

Bit bit bit bit, byte, byte
Kilobyte, kilobyte, bit byte kilobyte
Kilobyte megabyte, kilobyte megabyte
Megabyte gigabyte gigabyte gigabyte
Bit byte kilobyte megabyte gigabyte
Bit byte kilobyte megabyte gigabyte
Gigabyte biggerbite, biggerbite burgerking
Tuck in burgerking, bloodybig appetite, burgerking gigabyte
Bigmac megadeal, killerbug killerbyte
Lullaby night night (lullaby night night)

Glitterbug gigabyte, glitterball disco
Dancefloor set-alight, satellite, satellite
Cellulite celibate salivate sell-by-date
Corduroy trousers, purple tank-top

Internet interface, wintercoat cyberspace
Megaphone, megabyte, internet silicone
Digital silicone, digital silicone
Silicon Valley, pelican crossing
Pelican crossing, silicon valley
Silicone crossing, chilli con carne
Pelican valley, garlic dressing

Syllabub, sybarite, syllable startright
Vitamin vegemite gullible gigabyte
Megabug megabyte, jitterbug jitterbite
Sleepyhead gotobed killerbugs don't bite

Stalactite stalagmite superglue araldite
Erudite ammonite Eminem Acker Bilk
Tweedledum Tweedledee (Tellytubbies)
Sellotape, cellophane, Cilla Black Blind Hate

Technophile technophobe, techno notice
Dolomite dollar-bill, Dynarod dynamite
Dial-it-up get it right, digital kilobyte
Get it right get it right
Halibut uppercut, killer bee kilobyte
Get it right get it right
Megabyte gigabyte kilobyte alibi
Gigabyte megabyte kilobyte byte
bit bit bit bit
bit byte, kilobyte, megabyte, gigabyte
night night

A PINCH AND A PUNCH

a pinch and a punch
    for the first of the month
a clip round the ear
    for the start of the year
quite a bad headache
    for the first of the decade
a pretty nasty injury
    for the start of the century
an accident involving plutonium and uranium
    for the beginning of the new millennium

After the loaded software come the glitches
After the stains, the camouflaging lies
After the operation, the neat stitches
After the mistakes, the growing wise

After the claim, the contrary assertion
After the pride, the unexpected fall
After the empty promise, the desertion
After the porch, the charming entrance hall

After the drop, assess collateral damage
After the fact, the fictions that we weave
After the film is back, the new self-image
After the proof, the pudding we believe

After the crime, the full investigation
After innocence, responsibility
After the train, the platform's desolation
After the age of twenty-one, the key

After the Summer's green, warm shades of Autumn
After the death, the coroner's report
After the show, the gutter-press post mortem
After the cutting thrust, the barbed retort

After the national news, the regional weather
After the teletext, a full round-up of scores
After the arrow's head, the tail's feather
After the poem, the storm of warm applause

TAKING A LEAF FROM THE LATE
MERVYN PEAKE

When people die we put them in the ground
in wooden boxes. Not all – some we burn,
then keep their powdery remnants in an urn.
Such practices, I think, are fairly sound.
What we do next, though, leaves me disappointed.
We set their name in stone with some dull line:
"He Sleepeth Deep." "She Drinketh Heav'nly Wine."
"She Is At Peace." "He Walks With The Anointed."
But Mervyn Peake wrote his own epitaph.
His words were sweet and simple, fair and few:
"To Live At All Is Miracle Enough."
I like that, Merv. That's what I'd like to do.
I'd keep mine simple, too, and slightly clever.
My name, two dates, then: "Better 'Late' Than Never."